T0272268

LEARNING
ROOTS

On the authority of Anas Ibn Malik ﷺ,
who said that the Prophet ﷺ said,

"None of you truly believe until I am more beloved to him than his parents, his children and all of humanity."

SAHIH AL-BUKHARI

My Prophet Muhammad ﷺ is a picture book designed to be a child's perfect introduction to the Seerah. We sought to design a book that maintained a flowing narrative, aided by stunning illustrations that touch upon the main events of the life of the Prophet Muhammad ﷺ. This tailored rendering of the Seerah provides a broad foundation for your child, upon which they can build their knowledge and love for the Messenger of Allah ﷺ. The characters, events and details of the story have been carefully selected and simplified in line with the needs of the intended audience. The reference for both the events and hadeeth quotations are based on the authentic works, *Ar-Raheeq Al-Makhtum* by Sayfur-Rahman Al-Mubarakpuri and *Waqafaat Tarbawiyyah Ma'a As-Seerah An-Nabawiyyah* by Ahmad Fareed.

Published in the United Kingdom in
1441 AH (2020 CE) by
Learning Roots Ltd.
London, UK
www.learningroots.com

Copyright © Learning Roots 2012
Authored by Yasmin Mussa and Zaheer Khatri.
Illustrations, typesetting and layout by the
Learning Roots Education Design Service.

Notice of Rights
All rights reserved. No part of this publication may
be reproduced, stored in a retrieval system, or
transmitted, in any form, or by any means, electronic,
mechanical, photocopying, recording or otherwise
without prior written permission from the publisher.

Acknowledgments
The publisher thanks Allah, Lord of the Worlds,
for making this publication possible.

British Library Cataloguing in Publication Data
A CIP catalogue record for this book is available
from the British Library.

Printed and bound in China
ISBN: 978-1-905516-83-4

The Prophet Muhammad ﷺ was carrying a message and he wanted the whole world to hear about it. The message was sent by Allah ﷻ, Lord of the Worlds. Telling people about it wasn't going to be easy. But then again, the Prophet Muhammad ﷺ was no ordinary man.

Out of everything Allah ﷻ had made, the Prophet Muhammad ﷺ was His best creation. The perfect man to be chosen as a Messenger of Allah and to deliver the message one last time: Worship Allah alone, do what Allah likes, and Jannah will be yours. Simple words that made perfect sense. But this was news that some people just didn't want to hear.

Muhammad ﷺ belonged to a tribe called the Quraysh that lived in the city of Makkah. The Quraysh didn't worship Allah ﷻ alone. They worshipped stones, and they had been doing it for years. Their forefathers did it, their fathers did it, and they did it too. They didn't want things to change, even if it led to Allah's ﷻ punishment.

The Prophet Muhammad ﷺ climbed to the top of a hill in the city, called all the people together and said, "If I were to tell you that an army was about to come at you from behind those mountains, would you believe me?"

"Yes," they said. "We've never heard a lie from you. We've only heard you saying the truth."

"Then I warn you of a punishment of a great day," said the Prophet ﷺ, keen to keep the world safe on the Day of Judgement. The message was out. And that's when the trouble really began.

The Quraysh sensed that if the people of Makkah heard and accepted the Quran, which are the words of Allah, recited by the Prophet ﷺ, then the city would change forever, and they would soon lose control over it. "Don't listen to him," they said. "He's making all this stuff up. These are just old stories."

But the powerful words of Allah touched every heart that listened to them. Everyone knew deep down that these words were not lies, and that Muhammad ﷺ, the Messenger of Allah, was the sweetest man in the land who always spoke the truth.

"Say, 'there is no one worthy of worship except Allah', and you will be successful," said the Messenger ﷺ. Crowds gathered around him on busy market days and listened. Slowly, more and more people turned back to Allah, embraced Islam and became the Prophet's ﷺ Companions.

The Quraysh didn't like that at all. If telling people to ignore the message wasn't going to work, then they would have try scaring them away instead.

Leaders from the Quraysh hunted down the Companions and did horrible things to them. They stopped talking to the Muslims, they threw them in prison and hurt them. The Prophet Muhammad ﷺ arranged for some of his followers to sail away from Makkah to escape the pain.

The Messenger ﷺ himself was from the most noble tribe in Makkah, and was protected by his uncle, Abu Talib. With his uncle's support, the Quraysh could not harm the Prophet ﷺ in the same way. Instead, they hung up a notice on the Kabah, forcing all the other tribes of Makkah to boycott the Prophet's ﷺ clan by not buying or selling to them.

With little to eat and nowhere to go, the relatives of the Prophet ﷺ were imprisoned in their own town. Hunger starved them of their energy and dragged them to the mountain slopes of Makkah for three long years of hardship.

The harsh conditions weakened Abu Talib, and shortly after the boycott was over, the Prophet's ﷺ uncle died without accepting Islam. The Messenger's ﷺ sadness deepened when his dear wife, Khadijah ﷺ, the first person to believe in his message, also passed away shortly afterwards.

It was at this point that Allah comforted the Prophet ﷺ by sending him on a miraculous journey like no other in history...

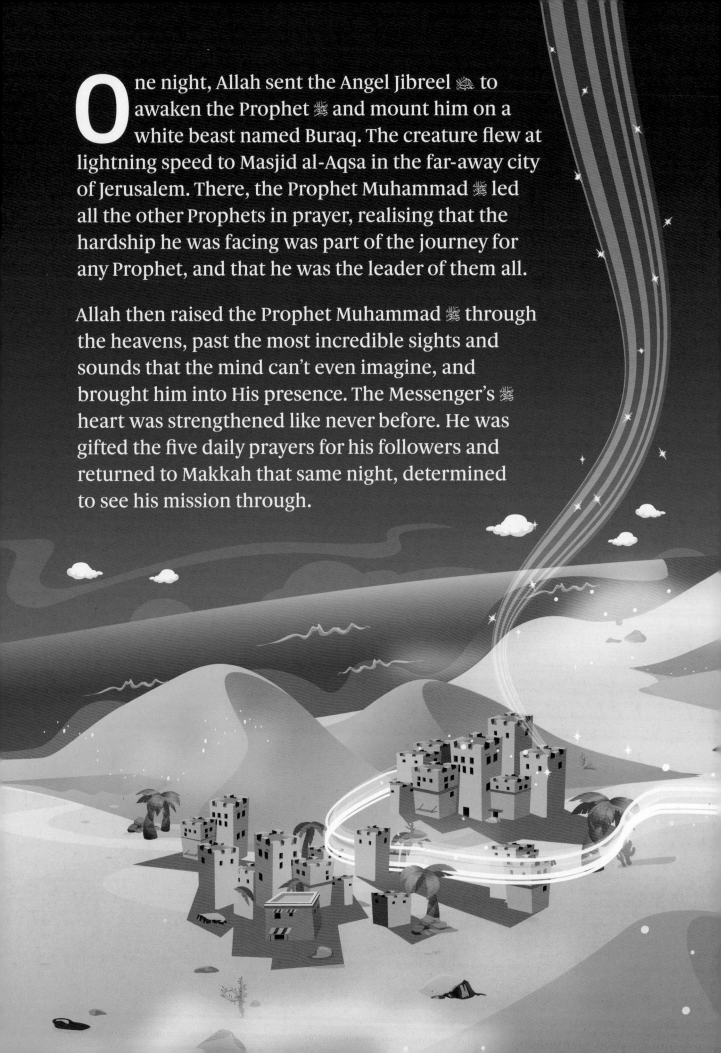

One night, Allah sent the Angel Jibreel ﷺ to awaken the Prophet ﷺ and mount him on a white beast named Buraq. The creature flew at lightning speed to Masjid al-Aqsa in the far-away city of Jerusalem. There, the Prophet Muhammad ﷺ led all the other Prophets in prayer, realising that the hardship he was facing was part of the journey for any Prophet, and that he was the leader of them all.

Allah then raised the Prophet Muhammad ﷺ through the heavens, past the most incredible sights and sounds that the mind can't even imagine, and brought him into His presence. The Messenger's ﷺ heart was strengthened like never before. He was gifted the five daily prayers for his followers and returned to Makkah that same night, determined to see his mission through.

The Prophet ﷺ knew he needed a clever plan if Islam was to thrive. So he sent a Companion to a town called Madinah to call the people to Allah ﷻ. The leaders of Madinah embraced Islam, held firm to Allah's promise of Jannah and longed for the blessed company of their great leader, Muhammad ﷺ.

Meanwhile, the Quraysh sensed an opportunity. With Abu Talib gone, the Prophet ﷺ had no one to protect him. They decided that now was the time to get rid of the Messenger ﷺ once and for all. The leaders of Quraysh gathered together and hatched a nasty plan...

ome men from the Quraysh crept up to the Prophet's ﷺ house under the cover of the night sky. They laid in wait to pounce on the Prophet ﷺ the moment he left his home. They waited and waited. But the Messenger of Allah ﷺ had already slipped out of Makkah.

"We'll reward one hundred camels to anyone who can catch Muhammad!" said the heads of the Quraysh. But it was too late. The Prophet ﷺ reached the safety of his new city, Madinah, where the Muslims showered him with a leader's welcome.

The Prophet Muhammad ﷺ built a masjid in Madinah and faced the Ka'bah whenever he prayed. Makkah was still very close to his heart and he hoped to return there one day. "From all of Allah's earth, you are the dearest place to me and the dearest to Allah," he said, facing his old city. "And if my people had not driven me out from you, I would never have left you."

But the Quraysh didn't just want Muhammad ﷺ out of Makkah. They wanted to stop the message forever and planned a surprise attack on the Prophet's ﷺ new city of Madinah.

The Quraysh charged out of Makkah with an army teeming with swords, arrows and spears. News reached the Prophet Muhammad ﷺ, who gathered a small army of Companions together and raced out of Madinah to defend Islam at the desert well of Badr.

The Quraysh sensed victory. The Muslim army was completely outnumbered. There was no better chance to wipe the message out once and for all. The Prophet ﷺ raised his hands to the sky and said, "O Allah! Please make Your promise come true. O Allah! If the Muslims perish today, You will never be worshipped again."

The battle began and Allah's ﷻ promise came true. An army of Angels swept down from the sky, striking fear into the hearts of the Quraysh. The Muslims chased the army, forcing them to flee back to Makkah. The Prophet Muhammad ﷺ had pushed the Quraysh away for now, but they were hungry for revenge. Their next attack was already being planned.

The Quraysh prepared a bigger, better and stronger army, ready to attack the Muslims at Mount Uhud, just outside Madinah. The Prophet Muhammad ﷺ was ready. The battle began. The Muslims charged at the Quraysh, pushing them back until they almost fled. But the army from Makkah thought of a new plan. They swept round from behind the mountain, trapping the Muslim army from both sides.

They threw a stone at the Prophet ﷺ, hitting him on the face. Blood poured down his cheek. He thought about the Quraysh and the pain they would feel forever if they did not accept the message. "O Allah, forgive my people," he said, "because they do not know."

The Muslims scrambled to safety up the mountain where the Quraysh could not catch them. They were badly beaten. "This day is for the day of Badr!" boasted a leader from the Quraysh. They wanted one last chance to stop the message forever. And to make sure they would get the job done, they called all the tribes around Makkah to join them for one last try.

urrounding tribes joined forces with the Quraysh on their march to Madinah. A gigantic army swarmed towards the Prophet's ﷺ city. But when they arrived at Madinah, they noticed something rather strange. A long deep trench blocked their way. "This is a trick that we haven't seen before!" they said.

The Prophet Muhammad ﷺ and his Companions had spent several tiresome days digging the trench, hungry and cold. They were camped on the other side and placed their trust in Allah.

The Quraysh attacked hard. They came from above. They came from below. The Muslims were shaken with fear, tested like never before. It was only a matter of time before the Quraysh would cross the trench. The Muslims couldn't hold on for much longer.

The Prophet Muhammad ﷺ cried out, "O Allah! Defeat the army! O Allah! Defeat them and shake the earth beneath them!" Wind stirred in the Quraysh camp. It became stronger and stronger, until it ripped tents out from the ground. Desert sand whipped their faces. They could barely open their eyes.

The Quraysh thought the wind would go away. But it didn't. They were pummelled for days on end, until they had no choice but to return to Makkah, defeated by Allah's ﷻ army.

The Prophet Muhammad ﷺ looked on, thankful for Allah's ﷻ mercy. He always wanted to return to Makkah, and with the Quraysh weakened, this was his chance. "Now we will head towards them." he said.

The Prophet ﷺ marshalled the Companions and headed secretly towards Makkah. The Quraysh were taken completely by surprise. The man who they drove out from their city was facing them with an army they had no chance of standing up to. "O Quraysh!" called out the Prophet ﷺ, "What do you think I will do with you?"

"We only expect good from you!" said the Quraysh. "Allah has preferred you above us!"

Deep down, the Quraysh knew that the Prophet's ﷺ message was true and that he was the kindest man they had ever known. "There is no blame on you today," said the Messenger ﷺ. "You are free to go." Just at that moment, faith settled in the hearts of the people of Makkah, and on that day, the Quraysh turned back to Allah and embraced Islam.

Allah's Messenger ﷺ shared the message of goodness with the whole world. He sent letters to every ruler and king in the surrounding lands, inviting them to Islam. It was his duty to Allah ﷻ, and he only ever wanted to please his Lord. He turned to the Companions and asked, "When Allah asks you about me, what will you say?"

"We will say that you gave us the message, you did what Allah asked you to do, and you advised us," they said. The Prophet Muhammad ﷺ smiled. With his duty fulfilled, he passed away, returning back to his Lord. He had changed the world forever and the message had been delivered.

Worship Allah alone, do what Allah likes, and Jannah will be yours.

What did you learn?

What did you learn from the character of the Prophet ﷺ in the story?

What did you learn from how the Prophet ﷺ treated and cared for others?

What did you learn from how Allah helped the Prophet ﷺ during his life?

What did you learn from the relationship that the Prophet ﷺ enjoyed with his Lord, Allah?

What did you learn from how the Prophet ﷺ was as a leader?

What did you learn from the Prophet's ﷺ words when he won over the Quraysh?

What did you learn from how much hard work the Prophet ﷺ put into his mission?

What did you learn from the Prophet's ﷺ attitude when things became hard for him?

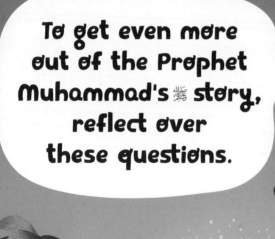

To get even more out of the Prophet Muhammad's ﷺ story, reflect over these questions.

Let's Raise
Great
Muslim Children

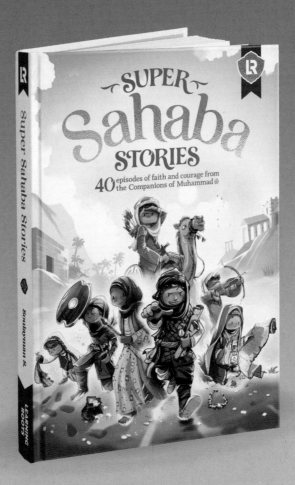

For the next level up, visit

LearningRoots.com

Worldwide Shipping